AMAZING FACTS AND TRIVIA

A collection of weird, wonderful and unbelievable facts to blow your mind.

Australia has in excess of 10,000 sea shores. You could visit another one consistently for more than 27 years!

Canada has the longest shore of any nation, extending north of 202,080 kilometres (125,187 miles).

Japan has a "train station" on a mountain top called the "Takamatsu Station," which is 1,800 metres (5,906 feet) above ocean level.

Iceland has no mosquitoes. The country's special environment and geology ward them off.

China is home to the world's longest wall, the Incomparable Mass of China, which extends more than 13,000 miles (21,196 kilometres).

Brazil is home to the Amazon Rainforest, which produces around 20% of the world's oxygen.

Russia is the biggest country on the planet via land region, traversing more than 17 million square kilometres (6.6 million square miles).

France is the most visited country on the planet, drawing in around 89 million vacationers every year.

Nepal is home to Mount Everest, the most elevated top on the planet, remaining at 8,848 metres (29,029 feet) above ocean level.

Egypt has the most seasoned known pyramid, the Pyramid of Djoser, worked around 2670 BC.

South Africa is the main country on the planet to have facilitated the World Cup in both rugby and soccer.

India is known for its different cooking, which incorporates north of 200 assortments of local foods.

Italy has a city called Venice that is based on 118 little islands, associated by north of 400 scaffolds.

Australia is the main landmass covered by a solitary nation and is the world's littlest mainland.

New Zealand has more sheep than individuals, with roughly 30 million sheep contrasted with around 5 million individuals.

Chile is home to the Atacama Desert, the driest desert on the planet.

Argentina is renowned for its tango music and dance, beginning in Buenos Aires in the late nineteenth hundred years.

Thailand is known as the "Place where there are Grins" because of the neighbourliness and inviting nature of its kin.

Switzerland has four authority dialects: German, French, Italian, and Romansh.

Greece has in excess of 6,000 islands, of which around 227 are possessed.

Spain is home to the world's second-biggest tomato battle, La Tomatina, held every year in Buñol.

Turkey is the main country that traverses two landmasses: Europe and Asia.

Mexico presented chocolate, chilies, and vanilla to the world.

Mongolia has the biggest sand desert on the planet, the Gobi Desert.

Belgium is known for its chocolate and waffles, however it additionally has more than 200 distinct sorts of lager.

The Netherlands is renowned for its windmills, however it likewise has in excess of 1,000 working windmills today.

Portugal is known for its stopper creation; it produces around half of the world's plug.

South Korea has the world's quickest web speeds, with a normal of around 26.7 Mbps.

Peru is home to Machu Picchu, an old Incan city set high in the Andes Mountains.

Denmark is viewed as the most joyful country on the planet as per a few worldwide satisfaction lists.

Estonia was the primary country to offer e-residency, permitting individuals to begin organisations online from anyplace on the planet.

Jamaica is the origin of reggae music, and Bob Marley is its most well known representative.

Hong Kong is known for having the largest number of high rises on the planet.

Singapore has one of the world's strictest regulations on biting gum, making it against the law to import or sell it.

Poland has a practice of naming each kid after holy people, and that implies many names are shared the nation over.

Iceland has a geothermal spa called the Blue Tidal pond, prestigious for its mending properties and shocking blue waters.

Vietnam is renowned for its espresso, especially its novel egg espresso, which integrates whipped egg yolk.

Finland is home to the native Sámi individuals, who have their own particular language and culture.

Cuba is known for its exemplary vehicles, as numerous vehicles from the 1950s are still being used because of exchange limitations.

Laos is one of a handful of the landlocked nations in Southeast Asia and is known for its staggering normal scenes.

Montenegro has a sound called Narrows of Kotor, which is quite possibly the most indented shoreline in the Mediterranean.

Zimbabwe is home to the Victoria Falls, one of the biggest and most well known cascades on the planet.

The Maldives comprises more than 1,000 coral islands, making it a top objective for jumping and swimming.

Cyprus has been partitioned starting around 1974 into the Greek-Cypriot south and the Turkish-Cypriot north.

Bhutan estimates its prosperity not by Gross domestic product but rather by Gross Public Joy, focusing on otherworldly and ecological prosperity.

Rwanda is known for its fruitful preservation of mountain gorillas and has a public park devoted to their security.

Colombia is the world's biggest maker of emeralds and is eminent for its gemstone industry.

Oman has a portion of the world's most seasoned known human settlements, with archeological destinations going back millennia.

Luxembourg is quite possibly the littlest country in Europe however has quite possibly the greatest per capita pay on the planet.

Sweden has a remarkable custom of "fika," which includes having some time off to appreciate espresso and baked goods with companions or partners.

Norway encounters a peculiarity known as the 12 PM Sun, where the sun doesn't set for quite a long time in the late spring.

Saudi Arabia has no streams; it depends on underground springs and desalination for its water supply.

New York City has more than 200 miles (322 kilometres) of sea shores.

Belgium has a larger number of palaces per square kilometre than some other countries in Europe.

Taiwan has a night market culture with over 100 night markets offering an assortment of road food sources.

Turkey has a remarkable type of wrestling called "Oil Wrestling," where contenders are drenched in olive oil.

Argentina is home to the world's biggest cascade framework, the Iguazu Falls, traversing almost 2 miles (3 kilometres).

Germany has north of 1,500 distinct sorts of brew, on account of its Lager Immaculateness Regulation, which traces all the way back to 1516.

Andorra is quite possibly the littlest country in Europe and has no standing armed force.

Sri Lanka has the world's biggest cut Buddha sculpture, the Aukana Buddha, remaining at 42 feet (13 metres) tall.

Nepal has the world's most noteworthy mountain and is additionally the origination of Buddha in Lumbini.

Ethiopia is the main African country never to have been colonised, protecting its antiquated culture and customs.

Fiji comprises in excess of 300 islands, with each offering novel sea shores and normal magnificence.

Gabon has one of the world's biggest rainforests, covering around 85% of its territory.

Vatican City is the littlest country on the planet, with an area of around 44 hectares (110 sections of land).

Monaco is the second smallest country on the planet and has the most noteworthy Gross domestic product per capita.

Bahrain is an archipelago comprising 33 islands, and its name signifies "two oceans" in Arabic.

Slovenia is known for its staggering Lake Drained, which includes a beautiful island and middle age palace.

Iceland is perhaps the most dynamic volcanic district on the planet, with around 30 dynamic volcanoes.

Panama is home to the Panama Waterway, which interfaces the Atlantic and Pacific Seas and altogether abbreviates sea ventures.

Zimbabwe has the Incomparable Zimbabwe Demolishes, the biggest old construction in sub-Saharan Africa.

Malta is known for its broad and very much protected middle age engineering and has north of 7,000 years of history.

Myanmar (Burma) has north of 2,000 Buddhist sanctuaries and pagodas in the Bagan Archeological Zone.

San Marino is the world's most established republic, established in Promotion 301, and is totally encircled by Italy.

Georgia is known for its antiquated wine-production custom, accepted to be one of the most seasoned on the planet.

Austria has a one of a kind practice called "Krampusnacht," where individuals take on the appearance of the legendary Krampus, an animal that rebuffs devious youngsters.

Mali is home to the city of Timbuktu, a verifiable focus of learning and exchange in the Sahara Desert.

Qatar has the world's most noteworthy Gross domestic product per capita and is known for its advanced engineering and extravagance.

Botswana is known for its different untamed life and is one of only a handful of exceptional spots where you can see the African elephant right at home.

Portugal has a remarkable type of music called Fado, described by its melancholic and heartfelt songs.

Romania is home to the Transylvanian area, broadly connected with the Dracula legend.

Jordan has Petra, an old city cut into pink sandstone bluffs, which is one of the New Seven Marvels of the World.

Singapore has a man-made island called Sentosa, which highlights sea shores, a gambling club, and amusement parks.

Laos commends the yearly Boun Pi Mai (Lao New Year) with a monstrous water celebration, where individuals sprinkle each other with water.

Lebanon has the most established ceaselessly possessed city on the planet, Byblos, which traces all the way back to around 5000 BC.

Armenia is the main country to embrace Christianity as its state religion, around 301 Promotion.

Malaysia has the world's biggest cavern chamber, Sarawak Chamber, which can fit a few enormous planes.

Iceland is perhaps the best spot on the planet to see Aurora Borealis because of its high scope and low light contamination.

Suriname is the littlest country in South America and has a populace that is a blend of various societies.

Chile has Easter Island (Rapa Nui), renowned for its huge stone sculptures called Moai.

Nepal has 8 of the 14 most elevated tops on the planet, including Everest, the tallest of all.

The Czech Republic is home to the world's biggest antiquated palace complex, Prague Palace, which traces all the way back to the ninth 100 years.

Bulgaria is known for its Rose Valley, where more than 85% of the world's rose oil is created.

Turkey has a city, Istanbul, that traverses two mainlands, Europe and Asia, and is a significant social and monetary centre.

Antarctica is the driest, windiest, and coldest landmass, and it is the main landmass without a local human populace.

Ecuador is named for the equator, which goes through the nation, and it has a landmark denoting the "Center of the World."

Switzerland is known for its nonpartisanship and has not been associated with any conflicts starting around 1815.

Samoa is one of a handful of the spots where you can encounter a day that endures 48 hours, because of its time region changes.

Croatia has north of 1,000 islands along its Adriatic coast, with the absolute most gorgeous and untainted sea shores in Europe.

Liechtenstein is a landlocked country with no tactical powers and is known for areas of strength for its area.

Sweden has a "Right of Community" regulation, which permits individuals to meander unreservedly in nature, pick wildflowers, and camp anyplace, as long as they regard the climate.

Australia is home to the world's biggest residing structure, the Incomparable Boundary Reef, which traverses more than 2,300 kilometres (1,430 miles).

New Zealand has the Southern Side of the equator's tallest mountain, Aoraki/Mount Cook, remaining at 3,724 metres (12,218 feet).

Chile has a tremendous and changed scene, including the driest desert, the Atacama, and the cold southern Patagonian district.

Colombia is eminent for its espresso, and the locale known as the Espresso Triangle is especially renowned for creating excellent beans.

Saudi Arabia has the Rub' al Khali, or the Vacant Quarter, the world's biggest nonstop sand desert.

Panama is the main spot where you can see the dawn on the Pacific Sea and set on the Atlantic Sea around the same time.

Finland is home to the "Place that is known for 1,000 Lakes," however in all actuality, it has more than 188,000 lakes.

Ghana is known for its vivid kente fabric, which has mind boggling designs and is customarily worn during unique functions.

Madagascar is home to lemurs, which are found no place else on the planet, and it has an exceptionally widely varied vegetation because of its disengagement.

Iceland has more than 200 volcanoes, and emissions happen on a normal basis each 4-5 years.

Slovakia has in excess of 6,000 caverns, including the absolute longest and most profound in Europe.

Moldova is known for its wine industry, and it has the world's biggest wine basement, Milestii Mici, which extends more than 200 kilometres (124 miles).

Andorra has the most noteworthy typical height of any country in Europe, making it an extraordinary objective for skiing and climbing.

Honduras is home to the Mayan remnants of Copán, which are known for their mind boggling stone carvings and stelae.

Albania has in excess of 400 kilometres (250 miles) of wonderful, to a great extent untainted shore along the Adriatic and Ionian Oceans.

Greece has an exceptional peculiarity known as the "Blue Caverns" on the island of Zakynthos, where the light makes staggering blue reflections.

Taiwan is popular for its night advertisements and is known for its air pocket tea, which started there.

Jamaica has the Blue Mountains, which are prestigious for their espresso and are one of the greatest mountain ranges in the Caribbean.

Cuba is known for its dynamic culture, including its brilliant pilgrim engineering, exemplary vehicles, and enthusiastic music scene.

Nepal praises the celebration of Dashain, which is perhaps the longest Hindu celebration and includes different customs and family social occasions.

Vanuatu is well known for its "property plunging" custom, where men hop from wooden pinnacles with plants attached to their lower legs to demonstrate their dauntlessness and bring ripeness.

Myanmar is home to the Shwedagon Pagoda, a brilliant stupa that is viewed as quite possibly the most consecrated Buddhist site in the country.

Brunei is one of the world's most well off countries, because of its broad oil and gas stores, and it is likewise known for its unblemished rainforests.

Lebanon is popular for its antiquated remnants, including the Roman sanctuaries of Baalbek, which are the absolute best-safeguarded Roman vestiges on the planet.

The Czech Republic is known for its wonderful capital, Prague, which flaunts a shocking middle age design, including the Charles Scaffold and Old Town Square.

Bulgaria has a practice of "Baba Marta Day" on Spring first, where individuals trade red and white yarn beautifications to represent the appearance of spring.

Ecuador is home to the Galápagos Islands, which roused Charles Darwin's hypothesis of advancement because of its remarkable untamed life.

Japan has a custom of cherry blossom viewing called Hanami, where individuals assemble to see the value in the excellence of sprouting cherry trees in spring.

Kuwait has one of the biggest oil reserves on the planet and is known for its cutting edge engineering and extravagance shopping centres.

Holy person Lucia is known for its staggering twin pinnacles, the Pitons, which are volcanic towers that ascent decisively from the ocean.

Estonia has a computerised society that permits its residents to cast a ballot online in decisions and begin organisations

Kazakhstan has the world's biggest landlocked waterway, the Caspian Ocean, which is bigger than every one of the Incomparable Lakes joined.

South Sudan is the most current country on the planet, acquiring autonomy from Sudan in 2011.

Sri Lanka is known for its tea ranches, and it is one of the world's biggest exporters of tea, especially Ceylon tea.

Zambia is home to the Lower Zambezi Public Park, which offers the absolute best natural life seeing in Africa, including elephants and lions.

Jordan is home to Watercourse Rum, a staggering desert scene frequently alluded to as "The Valley of the Moon," which has been utilised as a recording area for motion pictures like "Lawrence of Arabia."

Iceland has an interesting fountain called Strokkur that emits each 6-10 minutes, shooting high temp water up to 20 metres (66 feet) out of sight.

San Marino is quite possibly the most seasoned enduring republic on the planet and has been consistently autonomous since its establishment in Promotion 301.

Macedonia is known for its wonderful Ohrid Lake, which is one of the most seasoned and most profound lakes in Europe, and is an UNESCO World Legacy site.

Tanzania is home to Mount Kilimanjaro, the tallest detached mountain on the planet, arriving at 5,895 metres (19,341 feet) above ocean level.

The Dominican Republic is the site of the most established European settlement in the Americas, including the most established constantly possessed city, Santo Domingo.

Somalia has the longest shoreline of any African nation, extending north of 3,333 kilometres (2,070 miles).

Singapore is famous for its broad organisation of nurseries and parks, including Nurseries by the Straight, which highlights modern Supertree structures.

Rwanda is known as the "Place that is known for 1,000 Slopes" because of its rocky territory and lavish, green scenes.

Ethiopia is one of a handful of the African nations that has its own content, Ge'ez, and its own schedule, which is seven to eight years behind the Gregorian schedule.

Luxembourg has one of the greatest places of tycoons per capita on the planet and is known for its elevated expectation of living.

Hungary is popular for its warm showers, with numerous verifiable spa towns like Budapest offering recuperating waters and wellbeing encounters.

Liechtenstein has the world's most noteworthy centralization of monetary foundations comparative with its populace, and it is an unmistakable worldwide monetary focus.

Niger has the world's biggest desert, the Sahara, covering quite a bit of its domain and giving sensational scenes.

Belize has the second-biggest obstruction reef on the planet, the Mesoamerican Hindrance Reef, which is an UNESCO World Legacy site.

Papua New Guinea has one of the greatest degrees of semantic variety on the planet, with more than 800 communicated in dialects.

Ukraine has the Chernobyl Rejection Zone, the site of the 1986 atomic debacle, which has turned into a site for the travel industry and logical review.

Serbia is home to the world's biggest archaic post, the Kalemegdan Stronghold, neglecting the conversion of the Sava and Danube streams.

Guatemala is known for its Mayan legacy, including the noteworthy remains of Tikal, which was a significant Mayan city.

Oman has a special practice of frankincense creation, which has been utilised for millennia in strict and social services.

Costa Rica is famous for its biodiversity and has laid out a critical piece of its property as safeguarded public stops and saves.

Myanmar has the world's biggest number of pagodas and stupas, particularly in the antiquated city of Bagan.

Brunei is known for its lavish Ruler Omar Ali Saifuddien Mosque, which is a staggering illustration of Islamic engineering.

Bahrain is popular for its Pearl Jumping legacy, which was generally a significant industry and is presently celebrated in social celebrations and exhibition halls.

Mongolia is one of the thickly populated nations on the planet, with a population thickness of only two individuals for every square kilometre.

Jamaica is the origin of reggae music and affects music around the world, particularly through Bob Marley.

Vietnam has a novel drifting business sector culture, with merchants selling products from boats on waterways like the Mekong.

Switzerland has a practice of direct majority rule government, permitting residents to decide on different issues and regulations through mandates.

Estonia has a strong e-government framework and was the primary country to offer e-residency, which permits worldwide residents to begin and oversee organisations on the web.

Botswana is known for its effective preservation endeavours, including safeguarding jeopardised species like the African wild canine.

Taiwan is well known for its night markets, which offer a wide assortment of road food sources and tidbits.

Iceland has a geothermal energy framework that gives a critical part of the nation's warming and power.

Nepal is known for its assorted geography, from the fields of the Terai to the transcending pinnacles of the Himalayas.

South Korea has a rich practice of kimchi-production, with different territorial varieties of this matured vegetable dish.

Lithuania has a remarkable practice called " Užgavėnės," a pre-Lenten celebration known for its bright veils and elaborate outfits.

Papua New Guinea is home to the world's most different assortment of dialects, with north of 800 unmistakable dialects spoken.

Chile has a different environmental range, from the Atacama Desert in the north to the glacial masses of Patagonia in the south.

Jordan is known for the Dead Ocean, which is pungent to such an extent that swimmers can drift easily on its surface.

Sweden has an idea called "lagom," signifying "the perfect sum," which impacts Swedish way of life and plan standards.

The Czech Republic is renowned for its lager culture, with a long history of blending and one of the greatest per capita brew utilizations on the planet.

Peru has the Nazca Lines, tremendous geoglyphs scratched into the desert floor, which stay a secret with respect to their motivation.

Brunei is known for its abundance from oil saves and has a government that intensely impacts the nation's way of life and administration.

Malawi is known for Lake Malawi, which is one of the biggest and most profound lakes in Africa and contains an exceptional variety of fish species.

Fiji comprises in excess of 300 islands, known for their lovely coral reefs, clear waters, and dynamic marine life.

Bhutan is known for estimating its prosperity by Gross Public Satisfaction as opposed to GDP, zeroing in on prosperity and natural protection.

Kazakhstan has a one of a kind landmark called the Bayterek Pinnacle in its capital, Nur-Ruler, representing the old tree of life.

Ecuador is home to the interesting Galápagos Islands, where Charles Darwin fostered his hypothesis of regular determination.

Holy person Kitts and Nevis is the littlest country in the Western Half of the globe both regarding region and populace.

Greece has in excess of 1,400 islands, however around 230 are possessed.

Montenegro is prestigious for its staggering Straight of Kotor, a beautiful fjord-like inlet that is an UNESCO World Legacy site.

Cyprus is partitioned into two sections: the Republic of Cyprus in the south and the Turkish Republic of Northern Cyprus, which is just perceived by Turkey.

Malaysia is known for its assorted culture and food, with impacts from Malay, Chinese, and Indian customs.

Armenia has the world's most established winery, tracing all the way back to around 4100 BC, found in the Areni-1 cavern complex.

Andorra has one of the world's most elevated futures, on account of its exclusive requirement of living and medical care framework.

Angola has the Kalandula Falls, perhaps of the biggest cascade in Africa by volume and width.

Haiti was the main country to acquire freedom from European pilgrim rule in Latin America and the Caribbean, in 1804.

San Marino has the world's most established protected republic, with an administration framework that has been set up since the thirteenth 100 years.

Sweden is home to the Icehotel, a yearly transitory lodging made completely of ice and snow, worked in Jukkasjärvi.

Barbados has the exceptional differentiation of being one of a handful of the spots in the reality where you can see both the dawn and dusk over the sea.

Seychelles is known for its wonderful sea shores, especially Anse Source d'Argent, which is in many cases recorded as one of the world's most lovely sea shores.

Suriname is noted for its rich social variety, with impacts from native, African, Indian, and Dutch societies.

Dominica is home to the world's second-biggest bubbling lake, situated in the Morne Trois Pitons Public Park.

Nepal has in excess of 1,000 sanctuaries and sanctums in the Kathmandu Valley alone, making it a rich community for Hindu and Buddhist culture.

Palau has the well known Jellyfish Lake, where non-stinging jellyfish have developed, permitting swimmers to communicate securely with them.

Zambia is known for the Lower Zambezi Public Park, where guests can encounter strolling safaris and see natural life like elephants and lions very close.

South Africa is home to the world's biggest separately planned bicycle race, the Cape Town Cycle Visit, which draws in a large number of members every year.

Guyana is known for its staggering Kaieteur Falls, one of the world's most impressive cascades, situated in the core of the rainforest.

Slovenia is known for its pleasant Lake Drained, which includes an enchanting island and a middle age palace.

Namibia has the world's most established desert, the Namib Desert, known for its striking red sand rises and exceptional desert-adjusted natural life.

Nepal flaunts in excess of 240 pinnacles that are more than 6,000 metres (19,685 feet) high, making it a haven for mountain dwellers.

Finland has a custom called "sisu," which alludes to a remarkable mix of assurance, flexibility, and valiance.

Iceland has a public park called Thingvellir, where the North American and Eurasian structural plates meet and are pulled apart.

Vanuatu is known for its conventional "land plunging" custom, where men bounce from towers with plants attached to their lower legs as a transitional experience.

Ukraine has an enormous, extraordinary geographic element called the Carpathian Mountains, known for their biodiversity and beautiful scenes.

Belize is home to the Hol Chan Marine Save, known for its rich marine biodiversity and the popular Blue Opening, a monster marine sinkhole.

Taiwan is known for its beautiful Taroko Crevasse, a dazzling normal miracle with marble gulches, cascades, and climbing trails.

Chile has the novel Atacama Desert, known as the driest put on The planet, where a few districts have not seen downpour for many years.

Oman is known for its dazzling desert scenes and antiquated strongholds, which mirror its rich history and vital area on old shipping lanes.

The Bahamas has the world's third-biggest hindrance reef, which gives phenomenal chances to plunge and swim.

Liechtenstein is a little country with no military, and it depends on Switzerland for protection and strategic portrayal.

Malta is known for its authentic locales, including the antiquated city of Mdina and the Massive Sanctuaries, probably the most established unattached designs on the planet.

Honduras is home to the antiquated Mayan city of Copán, which is prestigious for its complicatedly cut stelae and sanctuaries.

Jordan has the old city of Petra, an UNESCO World Legacy site well known for its stone cut engineering and water course framework.

Cuba has a rich social legacy with impacts from African, Spanish, and native Taino societies, reflected in its music, dance, and workmanship.

Angola is known for its different environments, including the thick rainforests of the Cabinda Region and the parched scenes of the Namib Desert.

Sri Lanka has an extraordinary biodiversity area of interest called the Sinharaja Woods Save, which is one of the final tropical rainforests in the country.

Morocco is renowned for its dynamic business sectors, like the medinas of Marrakech and Fes, known for their mind boggling design and clamouring souks.

Botswana has the Okavango Delta, perhaps the biggest inland delta on the planet, giving an exceptional territory to untamed life and supporting a rich biological system.

Estonia is known for its very much protected middle age engineering in Tallinn, with its notable Old Town being an UNESCO World Legacy site.

Nepal has a different scope of dialects and ethnic gatherings, with more than 120 dialects spoken across its different networks.

The Philippines comprises in excess of 7,000 islands and is known for its wonderful sea shores, completely clear waters, and dynamic marine life.

Cyprus has old archeological locales like Kourion and Salamis, exhibiting its rich verifiable and social legacy.

Brunei is known for its rich Ruler Hassanal Bolkiah Mosque, which highlights great Islamic engineering and gold arch.

Gabon is home to the Lope Public Park, an UNESCO World Legacy site known for its rich biodiversity, including woodland elephants and gorillas.

Bulgaria has the Rila Cloister, an UNESCO World Legacy site known for its staggering design and frescoes.

Guyana is known for its special social legacy, with a blend of native, African, and Indian impacts reflected in its celebrations and food.

San Marino is encircled totally by Italy and has a special administration structure with a background marked by being a free republic for quite a long time.

Montenegro has shocking normal excellence, including the unblemished sea shores of Budva and the sensational scenes of the Durmitor Public Park.

Moldova is known for its wine locales, with grape plantations and basements delivering the absolute best wines in Eastern Europe.

Suriname has a rich social blend in with impacts from Dutch, African, Indian, and Javanese societies, reflected in its different celebrations and food.

Kuwait has the Kuwait Pinnacles, a remarkable design milestone highlighting turning perception decks with all encompassing perspectives on the city.

Armenia has antiquated cloisters like Khor Virap, which offer dazzling perspectives on Mount Ararat and are critical in Armenian history.

Jamaica has a rich culinary practice, including dishes like jerk chicken and curried goat, impacted by its different social legacy.

Togo has the Koutammakou, the Place that is known for the Batammariba, an UNESCO World Legacy site known for its conventional mud-constructed tower houses.

Uruguay is known for its great Montevideo shore, which includes a long promenade called the Rambla, extending more than 13 miles (21 kilometres).

Ecuador is one of the world's most biodiverse nations comparative with its size, with a great many biological systems from the Amazon rainforest to the Andes mountains.

Macedonia is home to Lake Ohrid, one of the most seasoned and most profound lakes in Europe, known for its remarkable sea-going species.

Lesotho is a high-height country, with over 80% of its property lying north of 1,800 metres (5,900 feet) above ocean level.

Seychelles is known for its remarkable monster turtles, which can live for more than 100 years and are local to the Aldabra Atoll.

Gambia is quite possibly the littlest country in Africa and is known for its rich birdlife, especially around the Gambia Stream.

Liechtenstein has a yearly "Liechtenstein Public Day" on August 15, praising the nation's freedom and sway.
Bahrain has the Bahrain Stronghold, an archeological site that traces all the way back to the Dilmun development and offers bits of knowledge into old exchange and culture.

Oman is eminent for its antiquated sea history, with conventional dhow boats utilised for exchange across the Indian Sea.

Yemen is known for its special design legacy, including the Old City of Sana'a, which is an UNESCO World Legacy site with particular mud-block high rises.

Malawi has one of the biggest and most assorted freshwater lakes in Africa, Lake Malawi, which is home to more than 1,000 types of fish.

Ghana is known for its dynamic kente material, which is handwoven with vivid examples and is generally worn during services and festivities.

New Zealand has a novel bird called the kiwi, which is a flightless bird and a public image of the country.

Mali has the noteworthy city of Timbuktu, known for its old original copies and was once a significant focal point of learning and exchange.

Portugal is eminent for its notable port wine, created in the Douro Valley and matured in basements in the city of Porto.

Sri Lanka has a rich social legacy with huge old locales, for example, Sigiriya, a monstrous stone post with frescoes and ruins.

Zanzibar is an archipelago off the shore of Tanzania known for its shocking sea shores, flavour ranches, and authentic Stone Town.

Papua New Guinea has the "sing" celebrations, where various clans meet up to perform customary moves and feature their extraordinary societies.

South Korea has a dynamic mainstream society industry, with K-pop (Korean popular music) and Korean shows acquiring worldwide fame.

Moldova is known for its lavish grape plantations and broad wine basements, including the Cricova Winery, which has underground passages extending more than 120 kilometres (75 miles).

Togo is known for its assorted culture, with different ethnic gatherings including the Ewe, Kabyé, and Mina, each with one of a kind customs and celebrations.

Iceland has a remarkable geothermal tidal pond called the Blue Tidal pond, which is renowned for its mineral-rich waters and dazzling setting.

Jordan is home to the antiquated Roman city of Jerash, known for its very much safeguarded ruins and great archeological locales.

Bhutan is famous for its conventional celebrations, like the Tsechu, where local people wear elaborate outfits and perform customary moves.

Vatican City is the littlest autonomous state on the planet, both concerning region and populace, and is the otherworldly and authoritative focus of the Roman Catholic Church.

The Middle Easterner Emirates is known for the Burj Khalifa in Dubai, the tallest structure on the planet, remaining at 828 metres (2,717 feet).

Greece has a rich old history, remembering the Parthenon for Athens, a notable image of traditional design and a vote based system.

Switzerland is known for its accurate designing and is home to a portion of the world's most famous watchmaking organisations.

Estonia has a practice of "computerised nomadism," being perhaps the earliest country to offer an advanced wanderer visa, permitting individuals to live and work from a distance.

Croatia has a lovely Adriatic shore and is renowned for its middle age towns like Dubrovnik, known as the "Pearl of the Adriatic."

South Sudan is known for its rich social variety, with north of 60 unique ethnic gatherings, each with its own unmistakable dialects and customs.

Georgia (the nation) is famous for its antiquated winemaking custom, with proof of winemaking going back north of 8,000 years.

Chile has the Atacama Desert, which includes probably the most clear night skies on the planet, mentioning it ideal for cosmic objective facts.

Myanmar is known for its brilliant sanctuaries, remembering the Shwedagon Pagoda for Yangon, a significant journey site for Buddhists.

Palau has the one of a kind Jellyfish Lake, where you can swim among non-stinging jellyfish because of their disengaged development.

Brunei has one of the world's biggest mosques, the Ruler Omar Ali Saifuddien Mosque, known for its shocking design and gold arch.

Sweden is known for its development in supportability and has aggressive objectives to become carbon impartial by 2045.

Malaysia is known for its multicultural society, with critical impacts from Malay, Chinese, Indian, and native societies reflected in its celebrations and cooking.

Ecuador is one of only a handful of exceptional nations that has both Pacific and Atlantic coasts, giving a scope of various marine conditions.

Armenia has a rich social history, with old religious communities like Khor Virap offering all encompassing perspectives on Mount Ararat.

Albania is known for its various Ottoman-time towns and towns, which highlight extraordinary engineering and a mix of Mediterranean and Balkan impacts.

Cuba has an energetic expression scene, with Havana being popular for its vivid wall paintings, music, and dance, especially salsa and mambo.

Benin is known for its verifiable importance in the slave exchange and is home to the antiquated Realm of Dahomey, with authentic destinations like the Regal Royal residences of Abomey.

Mozambique has perhaps Africa's longest shoreline along the Indian Sea, with delightful sea shores and rich marine biodiversity.

Niger is home to the Aïr Mountains, an UNESCO World Legacy site known for its special desert scenes and old stone workmanship.

Nepal has a rich practice of celebrations, including Dashain and Tihar, which are praised with lively services, dining experiences, and ceremonies.

Kazakhstan has the Tomb of Khoja Ahmed Yasawi, an UNESCO World Legacy site, which is a significant journey site for Muslims.

Iceland has one of a kind topographical elements like fountains, natural aquifers, and magma fields, making it a focal point for geothermal movement.

Lithuania has a rich social legacy, with customary people workmanship and specialties including elaborate wooden carvings and unpredictable winding around designs.

Tanzania is home to Serengeti Public Park, renowned for the Incomparable Movement, where a huge number of wildebeest, zebras, and gazelles relocate every year.

Singapore is prestigious for its effective public vehicle framework, including the famous MRT (Mass Quick Travel) organisation.

Mali is known for its rich melodic legacy, with customary instruments like the kora (a sort of harp) and the djembe (a drum) assuming a focal part in its way of life.

Gabon is known for its rich rainforests, including the Ivindo Public Park, which highlights great cascades like the Langoué Bai.

South Africa has the Support of Humanity, an UNESCO World Legacy site where probably the most established primate fossils have been found.

Palestine has authentic destinations like the Congregation of the Nativity in Bethlehem, accepted to be the origin of Jesus Christ.

Sri Lanka is known for its tea ranches in the focal good countries, especially in locales like Nuwara Eliya, which produce widely acclaimed Ceylon tea.

Georgia (the nation) has an extraordinary letter set and language that are particular from some other on the planet, with its own content.

Fiji is popular for its customary Fijian services and cordiality, including the "kava" function where a conventional beverage is divided between members.

Holy Person Vincent and the Grenadines is known for its shocking regular scenes, including the renowned volcanic island of Bequia and the lavish Grenadines.

Andorra has an exceptional mix of French and Spanish impacts in its way of life, reflected in its cooking, engineering, and celebrations.

www.ingramcontent.com/pod-product-compliance
Lightning Source LLC
Chambersburg PA
CBHW061533250726
48657CB00005B/2208